Assiniboia

BOOKS BY TIM LILBURN

POETRY
Names of God (1986)
From the Great Above She Opened Her Ear to the Great Below
(with Susan Shantz) (1988)
Tourist to Ecstasy (1989)
Moosewood Sandhills (1994)
To the River (1999)
Kill-site (2003)
Desire Never Leaves: The Poetry of Tim Lilburn
(with Alison Calder) (2006)
Orphic Politics (2008)
Assiniboia (2012)

ESSAYS
Poetry and Knowing: Speculative Essays and Interviews (editor) (1995)
Living in the World as If It Were Home (1999)
Thinking and Singing: Poetry and the Practice of Philosophy (editor) (2002)
Going Home (2008)

Assiniboia

Two Choral Performances
and
A Masque

TIM LILBURN

McClelland & Stewart

LIBRARY AND ARCHIVES CANADA CATALOGUING IN PUBLICATION

Lilburn, Tim, 1950–

Assiniboia / Tim Lilburn.

Poems.

ISBN 978-0-7710-5008-4

I. Title.

PS8573.I427A68 2012   C811'.54   C2011-906530-4

Published simultaneously in the United States of America by McClelland & Stewart Ltd., P.O. Box 1030, Plattsburgh, New York 12901

Library of Congress Control Number: 2011938746

We acknowledge the financial support of the Government of Canada through the Book Publishing Industry Development Program and that of the Government of Ontario through the Ontario Media Development Corporation's Ontario Book Initiative. We further acknowledge the support of the Canada Council for the Arts and the Ontario Arts Council for our publishing program.

Cover art: © Shutterstock
Typeset in Perpetua by M&S, Toronto
Printed and bound in Canada

This book was produced using recycled materials.

McClelland & Stewart Ltd.
75 Sherbourne Street
Toronto, Ontario
M5A 2P9
www.mcclelland.com

1   2   3   4   5   16   15   14   13   12

CONTENTS

An Argument IX

EXEGESIS

Turtle Mountain 3
Rupert's Land 4
Past Jordan River 8
Raids, Full of Night,
Practised with Its Blades 9
House 13
Bull's Forehead Hill 14
Island 15
Angelology 16
Bakkhai 17
Exegesis 18
War Preparations 19
The Boats Coop and Settle 21
He Announces His Devotion to Sara Riel,
Her Theurgical Action 22

ASSINIBOIA

Assiniboia (a masque) 25

SONGS OF CLARITY IN FINAL PROCESSION

A Song of Clarity 63
Beyond Jordan River, Going 64

Mill Creek 65
Avicennan Recital (A Spiritual Topography) 66
Gold River 68
What We Will Do 71
Moving Objects in a Pneumatic Way 72
Egyptian Boat 74
Hey 76
Port Renfrew 77

ANTIPHON

Tahsis, Northwest Vancouver Island,
Edge of the Uttered Land 81

Assiniboia

AN ARGUMENT

The voice speaking this will be eroded, male

"Assiniboia" was the name given by the Provisional Government at Fort Garry to the land formerly traded into by the Hudson's Bay Company, which it had called Rupert's Land and sold, along with the North-Western Territory, to Canada in December 1869, the theft that founds our nation. The HBC sale included almost all lands drained by rivers flowing into Hudson Bay, the Arctic Ocean, and the Pacific Ocean north of the 49th parallel, excluding the southern United Colonies of Vancouver Island and British Columbia. The name also indicated for members of the revolutionary government, Louis Riel and the others, a particular style of rule, an imaginal state, polyglot (Cree, French, Assiniboine, Blackfoot, English, Michif), local, mixed race, Catholic-mystical, which lasted a few months, late winter to early summer, 1869–1870, reappearing briefly in Saskatchewan in 1885. Both governments were destroyed by armies from central Canada.

Some introductions are in order, since many unusual figures appear in the land, an aspirational, theophanic land, that follows – Sara Riel, Grey Nun (Sr. Marguerite-Marie) from the late 1800s; Suhrawardi, twelfth-century Persian philosopher and contemplative; Calypso, psychopomp, keeper, and lover of Odysseus; Honoré Jaxon, classicist and activist from the old North West and Riel's last secretary; the Cabri Man, immense stone effigy on a valley floor in hills north of the confluence of the Red Deer and South Saskatchewan Rivers. This list of players is not complete; here the polis, this repeopling of western Canada, is more than the living and the human. All stand and sing, appearing alone or with others in the unwalled theatre of the poem.

It is surprising how many of the old imperial gestures remain still vigorous among us. One way to move against them, from the settler side, is to bring forward, in a certain insistent way, the occluded mystical imagination, chthonic, convivial, in the Western cultural tradition itself, and fix it to this continent by first allowing it to wander freely. The army that wins, indeed, is a mystical one. The poems gathered here are its armourer.

Dionysos:
Pentheus, nothing I say moves you in the slightest.

— *Bakkhai*, Euripides

EXEGESIS

A Stranger, early morning, lower reaches of the mountain

The first time I worked through here
– see how little I knew – first gorge
West of the Livingstone Range, I was calling
Into badger holes, poking sticks down the throats
For Irish monks.
Pitted, pine snow a vinegary bulge against wet rock
At 5,000 feet, burnt trees to the top,
Turtle Mountain, from Lost Creek Fire, sun
A fingernail scrape in bachelor kettle aluminum,
And through it, the mountain's pig neck and back
Appeared to move.
Now rain bloom bear-sways up
The blade of the north hump.
Dendrites – they lived in trees, another crew
Rode bulls.
Each would light candles below the slanting night of soil.
Sheep came down from the snowline.
The mountain, half of it fell away, 1903,
Seventy killed in the valley,
Northeast face, a diamond mark sickening between its horns.
The women stayed back
On the Pike Lake acreages, living out of converted grain bins,
Herding a common drawer of knives.
I came through here, Blackfoot country,
And took it up, the bad-angled company of dead people,
My ear slipped in and took the teat
In the bedroom of glaciers, it was looking for the Angel, the Twin.

Narrator, eroded voice, a valley of coulees, afternoon

—*//*—

Wolverine Creek de-caves, walks in its underwear, carrying a willow
branch, then sets itself in the wounds
of Last Mountain Lake, where pelicans are, papery breath
            swinging from their stomachs' glide.
And Last Mountain Lake gives what it's done, rehab notes, endless antibiotic
    dripfeed of weeds, all its clothes and shoes, to the Qu'Appelle River and
    the Qu'Appelle
lays its money inside the body of the Assiniboine (into its side), river cranking,
                        with an avocet's hitch,
from Fort Pelly area, Kamsack, town of Enterprise, from the widefaced,
testosteroned stare of the Minichinas Hills.
Most of our courage slants wrong.
West, the stone Cabri Man rustles in poked and stirred light on salt plains.
Medicine wheels (quiet, move slowly now), saged-in pits on lunged hills.
Suncor waste ponds rebound bearings of day lost at a supreme height,
near the Athabasca, where the river packs its staked ass north.
Wolverine Creek tucks its nose below its tail
and the night can lance in around it.

—*//*—

Suncor hired the lord who invented the guitar, a turtle-in-a-handbag
kind of daemon, cattle rustler, Man-with-a-Knife.
He slid his put-on-backwards, hoofy shaman-shoes
on the glass floor.
No one had ever heard of shoes
used like that before he did it, nose in the groin of the wrong way.
Idiot cattle followed.
Religion grew to his lip like salmon lice.
On one knee before air audiences, the yet again big tent,
dance show impersonations.

The swollen trident flew by this one's look into the water's neck.
A little underage, he carried his own cradle,
tucked in horsey blankets various moustaches, goatees, and driver's licences.
Hermes (some say), the beloved.
He gores strings heavily every night in trailers in all the camps
chasing chords, blowing hard on coals in Stones' songs, sweetening oil from
the sand.
He's seen moving in lamplight behind skin
windows in traders' sunk cabins at Île-à-la-Crosse, High Level,
                              Fort Chipewyan,
heaved over, tail risen, yet curving over his head, enpenned, inflamed
with attention,
tilting the old accounts,
back and forth, lifting them, tilting, his man-falling-from-a-building eye,
smoothing, smoothing the columns' glowing, swaying flows.
Memory is the sweetest part of his heart.

                    —#—

Stay close, up alongside.
Flanged rainclouds jackknife and wreck up in first air southwest
of Dawson Creek,
mile 0, the Golden Road,
diesels churning, eddying, motionless in motel side lots and in front
of the laundromat with showers;
the air's burnt coffee.
Muskeg swamps sulk north.

At Fort Nelson the two-year-old within his pack of dogs raises a head
beside a flag of Labrador tea in earshot of the high-school football field
five hours after the vanishing from the backyard, dogs liquid weaving,
movement-suturing him in.
3:00 a.m., the twenty-year-old woman,
well-oiled, passed out in the street,
shorts at half-mast.
Swallows carve something not seen
above Muncho Lake near the Lodge eaves,

lanks of air slithering away next to each flight curve,
hung meat cut.

—*—

People like small piles of smoke on the South Gataga River
wait for orange food packs to sky-drop,
ghostgang rain tumplines across the hip of the Muskwa-Kechika range
and over the water's ridged, flipping back.
Sour gas wells flare in wind pelt somewhere, somewhere near.
Force blooms a torn black front eating east.
Logging roads hack up by thickset washes, the float plane sways
through
bullfields of mountains
into the lowest layer where shale-backed, fossil-tagged dragonflies
scale and scrape air
and a horsefly is caught in the fold of my shirt, August
heat.
Loons, vowel-soaked,
their language expertly deboned
of consonant, have come to invent the thinnest possible dusk,
handsome cold-pounded to sorrow, so an obsidian razor leaps
at a bell rope falling the centre of us.
In the morning, after a night of their cries, three
come toward me.

—*—

The northern Rockies set their tables above the snow, this wedge,
granite and shale and rag of glacier.
Toad River, slate-milky —
armpit pain, ache in the jaw —
twists under us.
A marine fossil lodges in the north bank,
plume of a horn floating from front bulge to where an anus would be,
113 Mile Creek, saw marks at one corner, up a side, fireweed, underwater
grass milled to rust above stone.
Memory is the sweetest part of his heart, and he's been through here,

with his cattle, the shoe-trick god, nose to the ground,
with a pointy bag.
Horsetail clouds jackknife and wreck
up in wind sideswipe in the Muskwa-Kechika, mountains'
names kept away in beaded pouches,
mountains' names left behind in braided grass boxes.

A Traveller, wandering among ferns

Loss Creek, near the coast,
Scythes its polished wheat shovel at Leech River fault
Slewing bushels of quartz-like self-substantia,
Small, cut-faced berries of itself,
Quickly
Under the single-lane, railway
Tie bridge. In birdlessness.
Moments later a tarry flux
Handstands and cannons
Through the rub-silvered barrel of its own body
Five hundred feet over Sombrio beach.
The water drops, it tears.
Alders on the bank
Like crushed asphalt.

Out of clear-cut dusk, bears,
One, then another,
On the ridge,
Dipping down.

1.

Calypso, low-voiced, calm, alarmingly helpful

Go into exile up Douglas mountain, P,KOL,S, white-pointed tip,
Through the Indian plum forest, go at this delectating,
Setting pieces of pre-chewed food on dead leaves
Before each of your ten senses, your real body, its charcoal
Circles pooled in your old body, through the Indian plum forest
That sways its neck in a stanchion of rain,
Just as Beowulf drove hard into the wound-pits of the lake and won.
Take it up.
Plum flower odour descends from its rocking, royal carriages, the white
earrings, the chandeliers it wears mink forth
A rusted frying pan, "cat urine and watermelon rind,"
Neck boil of a smell.

—*#*—

Prince Rupert of the Rhine
Tolls and woozes ahead, taller than trees, onionly hipped,
Carwrecked and jewel-shoed,
In an elf flu delirium that humps all
This to a single quivering,
Lonely cavalier pressing the crumbling lamp
Of the underlit seventeenth century, its candlepower of moths
To his head.

—*#*—

But you, cher, you will see Indian plum draw into a syringe
Of in-swept breath its truth-delivered-from-the-thigh ghost
And plinth it in its own coasting palm and you will see, My Heart,
Oregon grape, deep in its mechanism, claw through a crease in rock
And rent a room in Vancouver on Homer,

Bed, dresser, do not disturb, large windows overlooking
The street, across from the Sally Ann, where it will see its own body
Standing on the pavement, looking up at the window (it *sees* it)
And the grape will be individuated by this hammerstroke.

—#—

Suhrawardi, clothed in sword flash,
In speech's flying horse mane,
Satin flower, Douglas' Blue-eyed Grass,
Could appear from the centre of the plum's neglected burn stink,
Or in Fawn Lily.
He could rise and float from the bright hall of the Book
And stand loose in the lily's gantry.

Or he could just as easily unsilo in high pass snow, Sentinel Pass,
Much farther east, four hundred miles, V-ing planks
Of wind-glued snow,
Up, alone, no animals and their sucking
Eyes around.

2.

The Traveller replies

Rockslide cloud over the pope's nose of the Olympic Peninsula
Its whale-coloured scrawl and the Pacific, and the rain
Pinches off three hundred yards above trees.
I'd discuss a politics of ghosts
Around any fire, any time, with You, Beer Princess, Sweet
Fin Flash of Theogony.
There are two ways into Jordan River,
Via late antiquity, snaking the twist of the aorta
Of scatted Neoplatonism
Or a portage, naked, next to, black bears,
One, two, ravening through salal.

Wool, rockfall of rain,
Skin under the eyelid of rain.
Someone could flick in
Just above the water from the sea,
His booming ocularity a bee-sized black jet.
He'd find snow souring the land,
He'd smell grease caking from drums
And below this something fainter
Under the burned car.
Odour of knapped tools
Below soaked sand,
Tools with clouds
Of slag from palms.

3.

The Stranger advances, twirling an ivy sprig between his forefinger and thumb, dreamily

May, first quarter-inch of poplar leaves
Let out a puff of horse flank, and people wheel back
Into aspens, wild rose at Half-boy's camp
On the east gradient of the Livingstone Range
Foreheading into the Porcupine Hills. Bees, big as bear cubs, space walk
                        around willow flowers,
Early brome flares through splintered ground.

Boy's dead since December
— slashes of movement at the gravesite, sixty people at dusk with shovels,
Wearing pieces of his clothing,
Legion tam, leather coat,
Ground too dry to freeze, filling him in.
The smell of his clothes in the northwest wind now
As the people who will fast bed in.
The wind drags snow down in skin sleds from the territories;
But first rain's grindstone, then

Buckskin, some-grass-burnt-away sky,
Then snow's herd shoulder.
Down from Single Pine, Dickie coughs around his red gut
Near the slapping blue tarp where (he says) he sleeps.
Carl hums smoke-rubbed to the face in the sternum.
The animals self-pry from the ground and swim closer
Their fixed masks flaked off the centre of night.

Sara Riel

Stone ships totter into Hudson Bay,
Calving off somewhere else,
Greyer than ice, with dipping needle compasses,
Astrolabes, theodolites,
These like facial tattooing.
People slip off tundra
In ceremonial dress, pinfeathers of snow coming behind.

You could turn a corner in an old house, believe me,
Which is your plumage, your liver, your song,
Potato field visible from the southeast window, the sudden, abdominal well
Axing upward, that old house, and there someone, or perhaps some trees
Or a slope perhaps,
Has laid out a long meal down a narrow pine table
With ends in separate rooms,
A meal that changes you as you eat it
Lifting its antlers in.
Log cities, streets of mudded snow, appear inside you,
Smoke rising.
Or you could go through raspberry canes
And devil's club, snowfences of starlight,
And sense a little lake of bobbing nipples
Made up of small candles, monk-gardened,
Under the heave of ground. So you are protected.

The first time they didn't eat at Carter's camp
A man with a bird's name jimmied a probe of voice-smoke
Toward the faces rising between their rib cages;
Then deer blistered and swam from bearberry and wild rose.
The moon chatters in the saucer of the bay,
The ships lift and grind and fall subservient and lift at anchor at Fort Albany.
Servile, as I've said, heavily gunned.

Narrator, his voice pebble on pebble, rolling down a grade

Two-thousand-pound hill with a gigantic cock. Times
A few hundred thousand. Teeming, dolphin
Necked, patched with a sand saddle, deuce of rivers
Cable link into each other's rattler's jaws in front
Of it, runaway
Current sand slab downshifting against the bluff,
Then mooching east. A heron works
The dusk, crackle of shadows.
Antelope.

The Traveller

Rattling undercarriage of geese over this rainmound shed,
Its smell of burning heater dust like drying barley,
Swampy walls held in a crib of whale jaw bone.
Fish punch into these walls, digging in
On night's paleo-currents.
Their eggs have been found in certain human ears.
November thump of salmon
Hums all rock.
Flickers thicken the dogwood
With shaking, stabbing their three-cornered fruit.
The woman-archon comes, pollened with intelligence,
Each second or third dawn, lays her cigarette on the bedside table,
Ash end out, draws back the sheet
And lowers her face.
Warm afternoons, to get free of the flu
Of rain, I worm into caves;
Greased hat of bats, grime shine of their skins;
Their ammonia smell almost rubs me out.
Driftwood slides off every form
I make on the beach, the tide takes it, I'll never leave.
Vines, violets, springs; a band tightens around this head.
Someone breathes down a flute needle rasped into swan wing bone,
Another has twisted coat hangers around
Bear shoulder blades and slices them through fires
To dog what speech splits across those lofts
Of white heave near his eye.
The marks say I won't leave.
Icebergs appear in the bays, waddling through the Spanish names.
Turkey vultures swim up
Over slab crests of stub mountains.

The Narrator, a voice like a black and gold cigarette lighter passed between dry hands

The radiator shop in Bellevue, the rusted gills.
Brown horse river loosening its rivets, thickening, flaring as it invents
A buckle east.
Cottonwood poplar buds, their semen smell;
The lip red, scarred flowers of cottonwood.
Dippers burrow through water
Their work a wind-frothed current of sparks.
A pair of harlequin ducks, blasé, remembering their high-school
                    locker combinations, bump the hillocks of fast water.
The blond ponytail of the cop
Talking to the middle-aged male speeder hauling a boat with a motorhome
                    through the 60 kph zone in Frank.
The rad shop in Bellevue.
Everything the Active Intelligence, satin-lined pod of the stare
                    of the peculiar creature.
The biker-run radiator shop in the Pass.
Old paint in popped tins, white, with dust
Mixed in, borne as seeds, behind the abandoned, purple, unoxygened house.
Tubers or iris bulbs of what could be faces, in-skinned there and there;
Moose browsed low willow,
Dimmer switch hit, limestone,
This one big lump, enucleated, that dribbled and cartwheeled
From that reptile mountain a hundred and a few years ago.

The Stranger and Sara Riel

To swim through this night in the river,
Dragon's insides, deeper into the cave,
Going below the surface and shunting through a hole,
Burning juniper held always at antler height, we waited for the hole
As it u-ed up shyly, then
Again we did this, and there it bloomed, bowed spine curve
Of the bison, opening its mouth, car,
Car, veering off the guardrail from the calcite.

The Stranger

Milkweed, milkweed, soft-toothed moons
burbling saxophonic inside; within, rising pastures
and cow bells,
milkweed, beside broken greenhouses of rivers, milkweed.
Milkweed, dissolved, re-skeletoned
with the sun's horned current,
milkweed, in itself, leap-igniting
as thirty-one-year-old Cyd Charisse in *The Band Wagon*
with the shark-chewed Fred Astaire, 1953.
In milkweed a pole of liturgically clothed cats, then
behind this, the palace with breasted pillars,
where everyone is heard.
The *ta' wil* of milkweed,
that machinery, is caress and proffering ambassadorial gifts.
The milkweed holds still, holds still
for the eschatologically optimistic hermeneutic of milkweed,
milkweed, in the mind of Joseph, sitting beside milkweed
near the path, dream-taxonomist, sizzling
eye-balcony in the electron microscope theatre
– milkweed is the campaigns of Alexander into India.
It is a feeding station setting out bowls
of meat and bowls of rice for the children of the town of Blairmore, Alberta.
Pillar of ideograms.
The books are laid out, the gold lettering appears.
In milkweed hangs a coat of chainmail from the Crusades
sewn by crying spiders.
The table is set, gold letters appear.
Milkweed, flowering yellow, with black beauty marks,
milkweed, milkweed, by the throaty, overcome, Romeoric greenhouses of rivers
that gruff and mood and lord their load of tonnes
of cut flowers of shadow farther east, north then east.

The Traveller, Breather, the Weeper, moving

Still, alone, for her, for her,
the ice torque on the mountain's neck moans
for Sara Riel.
The sound rustles in the Port Alberni channel.
Fish below, choral fold of breath above.
It was long, brain-rooted
legs of smells starting things.
It was scarves calling.

But also Ibn 'Arabi and Utah Phillips
slide summerly into each other, on the northern plain
above Dawson Creek,
their loaned tongues elide,
their loaned tongues fall through
one another, early snow on air.
The glacier, it must be remembered, please, the area above the trees, moans
                    surely and long for Sara Riel.

Ibn 'Arabi and Utah Phillips become instantly *single*,
meeting in air northeast of Prince George.
They themselves, alone in air, they, elected, ovation-tipped javelin,
                    they, flame's phronetic nose.
His voicebox of bull kelp.
His voicebox of Isaiah stone.
The two have pant legs caught
in the tops of trees.
They've wandered in from nameless
topographical maps with rivers in the northern Rockies.
Utah Phillips, Ibn 'Arabi,
each with a stalk of devil's club,
each with a black berry wand,

they follow the clover path
just forming, opening up now, moving north, moving north and east. North.

Sara Riel

Off Fort Albany,
Near the landfill,
The boats coop and settle
Glaciers on their decks and in their holds.
They darken, grow dusky, fold in their gigantic black feathers.
Against their chains, the ships tighten and collapse,
They tighten and collapse;
White moths around lights, ice stubs
Scuff in narrow valleys below water's cold electric whip.

May snow picks through the southern pass, Rocky Mountains,
Below Crowsnest tower, through aspen, chamomile; ermine
Chip through neck-broke grass along and across coal seams.
Weather wrecks in.
The ships lift and fall as if being breathed
By the bay,
Throbbing pale serpents in them.
Moon-waxed fur brightens into an organ of vision
On watching otter.

HE ANNOUNCES HIS DEVOTION TO SARA RIEL,
HER THEURGICAL ACTION

The Stranger

1879 or thereabouts, 1882, a back way opened behind the actual
Years, water pushed under and through glacier ice,
And down it, elongated, Hudson Bay drainage long priesthole,
Twohandedly, you lance forward a platter made of horn
On which reclines a volcano highrise, tipping, curtseying, of fruit,
No, wait, sorry, wait, better light
In the hall and the room you've just entered,
I see it firmer now, a bowl, sleeping
Putto of lung blood.
The well-fleshed, kneading, draped place,
Shack in the woods, in the claws of the trees,
In the throat of the trees, chimney-shaped, that house,
You go in.
The blood's a red bush now
And at its foot nesting quail.
You make this entrance,
Twice your size with feathers, insistent,
With precise, ludic feet
Often.
This is how you think.
The room, underseen, bricked away,
Quakes around its oil lamp,
Three days' ride north of prairie,
Here the spin of the world is cleaned;
Prie-dieued, one eyed by a steel crucifix, buffalo herd
Coat shag of lamped shadow, squeezing, bulking, pulling back.
Your room.
Snow racks down like a canyon wall
At Île-à-la-Crosse,
A snowmobile tilts back, fires on a spinal tread,

To bite toward the fixed
Core of a lake,
Headbeam swaying.
Across again the room, you haul
　　　– no choir to carry it voicely,
　　　　　　no choir –
And haul
A century of never-unmoving, fat-marbled hair.

ASSINIBOIA

Louis Riel, defeated by the army of Frederick Middleton, was hanged in Regina, formerly Pile of Bones, in 1885. But colonial wars, as it turns out, are long mythopoeic wars.

The action in the poem that follows takes place in the intermediate world of the creative, theogonic imagination, an unlimited democracy, where everything has franchise, including land forms, the dead, animals, plants, wished-for presences. The locale may be read as a version of the afterlife of Riel.

The poem borrows devices from the masque, John Milton's *Comus* in particular, but owes much more to Johannes Bobrowski's elegiac *Sarmatian Times* and *Shadowland Rivers*. The work may be choreographed for ten or more dancers.

Let this recital be applied to the wound.

ASSINIBOIA

A Visionary Recital

Drums and cello. They stop abruptly.

FIRST WATCH
A sit of poplars, Qu'Appelle River valley, near the elbow of the South Saskatchewan
River, June, golden crowned kinglets stab and scratch in last fall's leaves.
Poplars:
Our bodies, the perfume of the seeded body, quake-hovering
Below skin, chime of its odour, are
Mansion superimposed on mansion, useless, angling hallways
Of oiled seeing, lancing scent of this seeing.
We are daemon.
We are women.

The stupid pricks,
Those people should be buried with fire,
Let those Canadians, let them be dug in at a small slant,
Or slivered into the dorsal wall of a church,
Now and then again later be buried
With smoking logs tied to them.
Then let them visit the burning southern hotel
Of a cancer and put a leg through the floor,
Then they will come and look at us.
Regina kid circa early 1960s, thirteen or fourteen, appears from the left, stands in
profile, claps three times, then squares himself to the audience.
Kid:
So he, Riel – I nearly pass my insides out with this in my mouth – was a
    light sweat
Within air, northwest Regina, late 50s mid-60s – don't tell anyone this
Got wormed into me, bacteriaed in, lifted
Its antler in, are you fine with this? ok? are you? –
In the pre-hood nook of Albert-Scott,
Two decades before Piapot and Standing Buffalo lurch-grazed south

Shudderingly and in,
Around Dewdney pool, a grasshoppery stiffarm against the ribs
Of what everyone figured, a little believed ok,
But who the fuck thought belief then really, so figured then, figured,
George Reed pounding off tackle, drilling eight yards,
To be nothing, summer idling,
East of the Pop-in Tearoom, its orange-black tiger ice cream,
But also west to the Government Grounds,
Where there was still the scent of gun oil from when John Locke was read
    on toilets
  As servants counted their instruments for them, polishing,
  And even west farther to the barracks
Where they sharpened the rope. I confess this. I have been food
For ghosts. I apologize
For how I look.

Riel, on a hospital bed, attached to a hydraulic hoist, pushes through the stage floor,
splitting sod, polar rhizome thatch. Low drums. He is wound in ropes like strands of
kelp. Or he may be lifted on a mat by dancers from below. Dressed in black, but as a
patient, feet bare.

Riel:
Who won?

Kid (consulting a clipboard):
Eheh, well, let's see. Jansenists, Port Royalists,
Cartesians, Baconians, British empiricists,
Lutheran exegetes, and we walk in their air,
Utilitarians, anti-millenarians, kind
And deeply concussed Masons.
Wait, wait *(he runs a finger again down the list)*
No, no, that's it.

A light clicks on at a lectern behind the boy and a little to his side. An Oblate
spiritual director sways into the light. He taps down a sheaf of notes and motions
with his chin to Riel.

Director:
An Atlantic rises in his saying,
The words slice away at his mouth, ribboning it.
His naïveté before visions, his floorless lyricism, makes his route

Idiosyncratic, that is specific to him, and repels a philosophical
Deepening of it.
Taché sent me, Louis. And his love.
Poplars:
We are daemon. And childless.
We are women.
And dormer rooms opening in a grove we sway to mirror.
*Bull's Forehead Hill, facing the confluence of the Red Deer and South Saskatchewan
Rivers, appears at the side of the stage. It flashes back and forth, long strides, in
black, its costume flowing around it like wind through a cottonwood. The figure
stops, claps loudly three times.*
Bull's Forehead Hill:
To Him they are *all* alive.
The pickerel in the green vision river send notes to what people say
in their houses.
Grasshoppers piston in wild chamomile.
Horses, elk, wolf swim the river;
Sandhill cranes in ramshackle tonnage
Latch and hinge to the bend of the South Saskatchewan River north
So they slick into torn grain fields near Batoche.
Riel turns slowly, stopping at each of the cardinal directions, rocking on fieldstone feet.
Riel:
All of it pressed and swivelled in my mouth,
Tumescent disc, armed galaxy, the continent's shining polity,
Wheeling itself through clouds of cranes,
That jerk down, dropping, multiple machine gives, as sloughs glint up,
The lift of a three-foot continental wedge of land moved with slack
Circularity in my mouth.
Whooping cranes and sandhill cranes sluicing in.
Kid:
We thought he was hanged in Grace Haven
Which made that place off-the-scale bomb-tricky, slammingly granny-tied,
We knew it smelled of acid in old batteries in there,
The unwed and dead, banged, hanged, how lonely can you get?
I nearly said Grave Haven, you know, eh.
Swinging in the nettle shade of those girls and their

Crepe-wearing, burnt wood, crackling, Sally-Ann keepers.

Poplars:

In a side-world, a world-house jacked by pneuma feet and hands

Sturgeon nose into a curved mist

In a human skull, nurse to the palm of a sung Assiniboia,

As a deer puts a hoof through lichen into sand, fireflies clouding, sweeping out.

A buck clacks its antlers along white trees, ribboning dusted bark.

The prickly pear does not bull-ride the hills but holds their reins.

The preoccupied grass under the river all votes one way

Below sandhills east of the river.

Kid claps twice.

The sloping rope was a stole around his neck, dead fox.

They must have lifted his beard to home or seat that shadow in.

The fox, raising its head, turned it, opened its mouth, lifted the beard.

Poplars clap once:

Horses, elk, wolf, deer swim the river,

Grasshoppers, mosquitoes, veil over after;

They trail the ford of the Qu'Appelle, then nose to tail nudge out to
    Batoche.

Sandhill cranes in slithering tonnage

Touch out the bend of the South Saskatchewan to the north

And twist

To wreck down into licked barley scrips below the Batoche

To St. Isidore Road.

Long pause, figures stand motionless, then the cello builds, becoming a flock of crows bunching and tearing apart in fall. The stage empties.

*Cranes circling in thermals. The Battle of Batoche unfolds below. Gigantic flashing
panels of cannon smoke, blurred men running, projected on the walls.*
Cranes:
Under us, snap of noon rifle fire,
Slapping, warehouse doors end-zoning on cleated wheels.
Middleton heaves to his horse, o-ring smoking,
Tilting at the slant of his medals,
And jerks forward, asphalt-stripping machine.
*Riel, whirling across the stage, wind-pushed forward and lifted slightly, then set down,
then lifted, then put down on sandstone feet.*
Riel:
A Copernican weightlessness and giddy gigantism
Swayed out in my chest, and I see myself lean under it
To find the nipple of rest.
Orangemen slide along their Springfields,
Gracile *Homo sapien* beauty.
They snick through trees.
I pillow-talked through night for a concordat
With candyish planet angles, whittled to gleam Jerusalems,
Put out my tongue for a single ace from a sage-rubbed chair of Peter,
So we might buffalo among them our greased, beaded bulletry.
*More battle scenes, old photos, floating like cinema ghosts, stampeded ghosts, sweep
across the walls. They lessen and fade away and cease.*
Long pause.
An extended draw on the cello, note blackening, a cottonwood leaf in November.
Riel exits.
*Bull's Forehead Hill claps three times slowly, then advances from the back of the stage.
He looks down, then up.*
Bull's Forehead Hill:
Damp ribbons up from all five coulees
Feeding into Thunder Creek valley
To nose the udder of Kettlehut Marsh.
The Red Deer River's breakfast fire smoke crawls upward
And loses weight,
The plain stiffens, stares out

To the Bearpaw Hills,
    Eagle Hills.
People trade this and that along the rosebushed South Saskatchewan,
You hear the clip of quills against tin plates.
I listen for the rivers, their otter tails.
I listen for fish touching in the water.
Human stone effigy embedded in grass near Cabri Lake, thirty yards, head to toe,
twenty miles north of Bull's Forehead Hill and the confluence of the Red Deer and
South Saskatchewan Rivers. This figure lies away from the others and lower, at the
level of the audience. He unpeels from the floor and climbs to the stage.
Cabri Man:
The sky, snow geese circling
Sloughs, night, night-meat, heavying and bearding in.
Listen: horses ford the river
Near Estuary turning hard to Batoche; they'll cross again in single file
    farther up
At St. Laurent, horses rising and falling in the flow, then
Hoof-click on small stones.
Sturgeon move their skins against the current, that bark-peeling sound.
That town is swallowed, that Batoche, tractored out, that Batoche.
Then beaver gruff smell in fog booms up from the valley,
Wild mint in this valley,
Cranes and pintails; bald eagles, salmon
Boned, reeds inching to yellow,
Muskrat mud thick in creeks,
Burrs and dock scuff along suncut banks of the South Saskatchewan,
Mosquitoes, blue-ribbed, rotor-thud in saskatoons
Grasshoppers piston in mint and pigweed, their hiss.
Pause. The effigy claps softly three times. Cello rises in an interrogative lift.
So that girl, Sara Riel, I just heard her rustling over there, near
    the dogwood;
So she's back in the family cabin, four hundred miles east, southeast,
Poplar walls smelling of mushrooms,
Cabin joined at the hip to a three-quarter dome of willows
                    at Red River Settlement
And she's talking

Slowly, as September snow falls, falls to her grandmother, supper
Done, dishes propped on a spruce board along the wall,
Cook stove plinking, cooling down, Henry Jackson
By for pie –
   geese sling back to the river from
          those cut fields near Gabriel Bridge, clawed feet rucking water skin –
Sara undoing her braids,
She talks after nine and later as her grandmother
Fixes the lamp.
Sara Riel slaps her hand twice on the scrubbed pine table.
Sara Riel:
I saw a wave over the prairie, I sucked my lips for it
To wattle down on my hand's roof,
A hum above sharpened grass
Like dragonflies, like grasshoppers,
Like July bottomland mosquitoes, but not coming
From any body or from my body, deep thousands deep, three thousand
   miles, I
Believed, wide. It was thinking about me.
You could see spiders like flint when you shake the rattle
Ride in that hum.
The cows muffled off into poplars in
The southeast this afternoon
Grass obese, a slump, stump of old sky
There.
I heard the muskrat squirm, saddle-leather-creak, into their mud.
I heard flickers scrape through leaves.
Her maternal grandmother, Marie-Anne Lagimodière, replies in Cree, dry grass in wind
sound (the first lines of Flute-Bearer):
pêyak ês ôma ôtênaw êh-misâk, êh-mâh-mêtawêcik, êh-môtocik. kîtahtawê
   pêyak awa iskwêw pakwâtam, êh-kitimâkêyimât osîmisah.
   "nka-sipwêhtahâw; ta-kakwê-uhpikiw," itêyihtam.
   êh-tipiskâyik, sipwêhtêw, êh-tapasît.
Dans la nuit, elle a parti rapidement.
Sara Riel claps once.
Sara Riel:

35

When I came through, cleaving northwest
On a living curve, snakehead whip
Between the rivers,
Above the hiss of my red-runnered sleigh,
Between the shake of rivers,
Some Poundmaker boys shouted to me they
Could hear animals
Goring air with the horn of their voice
Talking there, white tail, raccoon, fox, all
In poplars, snowberry,
To one another and I could gooseneck
My own tongue through that air too,
Clear as a well.
Coyotes savour down
Outside our walls. They whuff and lick
The songs coming out.
The reverberant ones – (Dickie, in tarp-rattle,
"The Walking Song" or Leo the Plume "The Woman's Song") –
Fold out along the ground and the
Coyote roll and roll on these songs,
Nipping the back legs of each other,
Lying down in the dirt, twisting their backs into the good chicken bone
Slick salmon skin smell.
Sara Riel's grandmother:
Flute-Bearer boy went into the wilderness,
Flute-Bearer a parti dans un désert,
For a magpie wife.
   (the coyote yelp and circle)
Henry Jackson:
He opened into an old arrow, he
Dragonflied into a stick, he jumbled and clouded, particles flowing
Into a woman, a clever female mountain of crows;
He went there stilting on the ends of his arrows,
He went right through the front door in dwarf moose, in deer, in buffalo,
As a purple-mouthed arrow,
Knocking first, wiping his feet, falling in.

Sara Riel claps twice
Sara Riel:
That boy was quiet for ten years
And the silence spread the shadow of a bird,
American robin, on the grass and became
Poplar leaves falling and the push of frost.
Sara Riel's grandmother:
The story goes there was this big town where they always had contests and
ate each other. The Lord showed this to me and put this in my hand.
Poplars:
O, we know that place.
It was called the Hudson's Bay Company.
Then later the Capital of Cigars.
(general laughter from all on and off stage)
Sara Riel's grandmother:
Then, at one time, a certain woman took a dislike to this, because she loved
her little brother.
kîtahtawê pêyak awa iskwêw pakwâtam, êh-kitimâkêyimât usîmisah.
Parce qu'elle a aimé son petit frère.
Henry Jackson:
"I shall try to take him away from here; I shall try to have him grow up," she
thought. In the night she went away, fleeing.
"Perhaps since my father and my mother have been killed, I am now alone
with my little brother – perhaps if there is another mass contest, I now shall
be killed," she thought; that was why she went away.
Grandmother:
After two nights' journey, she was at a place where the land was good, with
woods everywhere.
Poplars, clap twice:
And a river mudded there, longhaired, practised in sleep.
And they traded lightning-sight of humming-
Bird breast for a half-hour of thinking
About Robinson Jeffers and Teresa of Avila and
They traded a muskrat's smell for the
Shadow of a Canada goose abandoning its utter
On grass and they traded this for wheat in a laundry basket,

Eight-dollar wheat and this for an inch of moving water
And this for a new fan belt, Massey-Harris.

Pause, individuated darkness rises in speakers. They disappear. Drums, which become July thunder, which turn into a sound of hoofbeats on droughted prairie.

THIRD WATCH

Oblate, a few beers down:

Jesus Christ, what have you dug from under your fingernails, looks like old Rupert's Land. I catch night smell of water for miles, there's a deer lifting its head in Rachot's meadow, raccoons moony in poll barn lofts. Louis, Louis, Louis, there in your hands, look, what's that you got now there wound up in that delicious red cloth? *(Riel opens the red cloth, magpie feathers, sage, a twist of June sky, a mammoth footprint, eagle flight with marks of glacier ice having moved on it).* Louis, man, listen, your hands, wash them. Hey, hey, you've put your head in the mouth of particularity on this one, snuck your paws into the pants of the lefthand occult signs of partiality. Nyuk, nyuk. Bishop'll have to move you to a new parish. A joke, a joke. Hey, well. Look, dear guy, think of a kind of globalism of affect, a downtownism, which, in a strange physics, is universality and, for you, an elevation.

Your neck is bruised. Cut words black

Your lips.

Riel:

Long walks in the prairie of this cloth

Is a sung land.

I thought of here on the North Saskatchewan, near St. Antoine de Padoue,

roses, of broad rooms in which our feet

Are set, a cantable place.

Atoms reassemble, shaken in a dish, a clutter

Of bees, motes in a voice, tumblers in a wall safe,

Assiniboia bulks out of the brown ground

In the robe of the brown ground.

Riel and the priest quickly put on masks, pelt and leather, snakeskin, feather and antler, Riel part-man, part-deer, both in triumphant therianthropism, and begin to weave in a thick, lunatic dance that lasts a good while. Drums and cello rampant throughout. Riel suddenly stops. He claps three times quickly.

Riel:

I saw the purple biretta, it disappeared.

I saw the purple surplice disappear; it took

Some time to fade away.

I saw the purple robe of the postulant nun disappear.

My face bruised out of Mistasiniy erratic,

I walked out of the temptation to purity in the pit of liberation.
Riel and priest leave.
Henry Jackson (claps twice as he walks downstage with speed):
He sent me down a throat of light
And I'm back with
The language of six-yard topsoil,
Which lumps up in me
A breaching fish.
I am the utterance of movement.
I've been tyned by the current
I twist on the tynes
And my name slides away;
I am Honoré.

FOURTH WATCH

Kid wanders on stage, scratching his shoulder, looking back; he claps three times slowly.

Kid:

It's dead quiet

here now but I know

I heard a grimy sawing on a fiddle,

Like a cookfire going out,

A fire for warming beans or Chef Boyardee, smoke

Beanstalking, starving, swaying west of Pinkie

Out there in the prairie toward those Dirt Hills, the Coteau.

What the shit happened there?

But the flats are clean now.

We'd go over to the Pelletiers after breakfast

And haul out John, maybe his sister Lynn would come, maybe

Marie and Rhoda, and we'd cut through the Guvs,

Ripping through caraganas,

John ahead a quarter mile, those days, those days.

George Reeding, you know, through sticks

And behind Luther

And with the dogs be at the wind-purpled creek,

Greasy with muskrats, jump-eyed with weeds around dumped asphalt

And concrete, we had a giant steel water tank, six feet, eight feet

Acetylened down the middle we cracked ourselves to get it on the water,

We slopped back and forth, Wascana Creek, horseless, spearing muskrats,

Surveyor lathe swording down Pictish weeds.

Boy disappears.

Poplars:

Wind, December, chaffs over fields and roads.

You can hear pucks plink on outdoor goalposts,

Car tires click on ice.

Bull's Forehead Hill claps quickly four times, building in intensity and enthusiasm.

Bull's Forehead Hill:

Sturgeon lead down in the South Saskatchewan,

Ice a leaning shadow

Clay bottom scooped by the carded current.

Now magpies will coast or argue or float from a tree

A tail feather
For an afternoon of being sung to
From Heidegger's "The Question Concerning Technology"
In sun on wind-hardened snow.
And now wolf willow berry, the breadmaker
And the horn-spoon watch the fire.
And now Zwicky's *Lyric Philosophy* will glide
Across the table
A flight feather of shaped Incan quiet
For a whisper in the ear from the wolverine.
Sara Riel claps twice:
I left the convent at Île-à-la-Crosse twenty-eight days ago
Moving east, sibilant on mucus of rawhide, east
Through sick snow,
Then suddenly in moccasins.
My malletted lungs lifted in wind, a red,
Weeping web.
I hung the engorged cords with their wind across snowberry and moved.
St. Teresa of Avila's whispers wadded through me to the neck of the bottle
Wicking what blood plushed up there.
Poplars and Honoré Jaxon, each taking a phrase:
They never got around to it,
The Orange dicks,
Moving objects around on the ash-banked floor
Of the church at Batoche, lifting them from snow come through the roof,
        webby
Instruments
Of the state,
The tongue's girder arrangement for a sung Assiniboia,
Land-inside-land, scored land,
Nor did they feed or pay out what was for them
Windless groin to the violin.
Cabri Effigy, two claps:
Lie down, everyone, lie down
The barns flicker out in the
Hills and in the coulees and in

The flats, no yard lights, I tell you, even if you drove all night,
Tank emptying two and a half
Hours northeast out of Medicine Hat.
Lie down here in the grass, there's a stone, buffalo grooved,
Snow worked around it,
There are coyote, cougar, elk, snow bank-
Ing them in.
Farm yard lights loaded their wagons and creaked
Out two or three weeks ago,
Half-ton boxes full of lampwicks, coal crumbs, and gramophone cylinders,
Caruso's voice inside peaking, then grinding down
In packing felt.
The drum cups some sage to the cougar
And the cougar fiddles this into a five-ounce round of fire
Which it carries at the tip of its teeth to the top of Bull's Forehead Hill
Then another cat up another hill and another fire,
Another hill, another fire
North into solid night.

A single long stroke of the cello bow.

Sara Riel:
Dry snow clatters along hayrakes
Crocheted together on Little Pine's reserve
On half-worked ground, grown in ground.
They've killed or set forests on fire inside the heads of everyone,
The Ottawa cigars and the NW Mounted Police.
A snowy owl cutlasses over drifts,
I heave in birch shoes through snow
To the small of my back
Dragging the cape of debris from
The night both lungs exploded,
Wasp nests touched by a torch.
I had been leading the herd of the choir,
Schola was in me, cresting, breaking curl, I pulled with others and alone
In a squealing leather harness,
The choir's plate-footed voices churn behind me,
Up through passes, the Yellow Head, Kicking
Horse, I had been singing, I was singing.
Both lungs bleed now into tubes
That empty at my ankles.
The furnace of Jesus' heart
Swims before me in the storm
And I compose myself before it
Then reach in and pull out
A burned mouse.
I buried my first name in convent snow
At Île-à-la-Crosse.
We had only lettuce
That first fall, potato
Crop's neck was cut.
Nothing can stop me
From seeing my brother
Before whom Big Bear
Speaks tonight,

Small puff of the cold of himself,
Into his face
In Prince Albert
Under lamp-sigh
In Dumas' house,
His moulting light.
She leaves.
Riel, in another place on stage two seconds later, not seeing his sister, claps his
hands twice:
They are all alive to Him.
Some men later from Gabriel's cavalry
Went forward under slabs of turf,
Small trees waving along their backs,
From Gabriel's men they went,
Out of our bleeding side,
To smell and kiss the lip of what had listened toward us then,
In the rifle pits in the used-wax smell of the church.
And some went to the river to draw
Coins from sturgeon's mouths, massaging the fishes' throats
In lionish current,
And some shook blond musket balls
From wild oats
And some dressed entirely in August
Fescue sleighed ahead to get from safekeeping
White-tails the "Declaration of the Peoples of Rupert's Land
And the Northwest," 1869, stamped with their slots,
And some beaded the wind
And some chewed the leather of wounds
So we could wear them to walk back
And some touched the noses of horses
So the animals would not be insane but remain musical
And one woman rolled from her skirt
The bell from Batoche church
Far out on the river and when it boomed over watersmoke, the dead unstuck
And pressed against ice's undershelf
And some went into fallen poplar leaves

And sent money from there back home
And three went to Montana to wait
And five took up the art of goats in the eastern Rockies
And six forded the river as seven-foot wolves
To work down to Big Bear's vision hill
Near the long stone man at Cabri Lake.
They took up lookouts at the tips of ferns,
Raising daguerreotypes of their lost children
Peeled from lockets
As bullet shields
And some rolled back the ground and walked into the cavity,
And erected kitchens
And waited in the present ground for fire
To split them open.

The Cabri Effigy lifts up and recites "The Revised Bill of Rights. . ." in English, French, and some Cree. Music weaves through this recital its weather. Drums and cello.

The Revised Bill of Rights as Drawn by the Executive Council of the Provisional Government at Fort Garry, 1869

I. That the Territories heretofore known as Rupert's Land and North-West, shall not enter into the Confederation of the Dominion of Canada, except as a province; to be styled and know as the Province of Assiniboia, and with all the rights and privileges common to the different Provinces of the Dominion.

II. That we have two Representatives in the Senate. And four in the House of Commons of Canada, until such time as an increase of population entitle the Province to a greater Representation.

V. That all properties, rights and privileges enjoyed by the people of this Province, up to the date of our entering into the Confederation, be respected; and that the arrangement and confirmation of all customs, usages and privileges be left exclusively to the local Legislature.

XVII. That whereas the French and English speaking people of Assiniboia are so equally divided as to number, yet so united in their interests and so connected by commerce, family connections and other political and social relations, that it has, happily, been found impossible to bring them into hostile collision – although repeated attempts have been made by designing strangers, for reasons known to themselves, to bring about so ruinous and disastrous event – and whereas all the troubles and apparent dissensions of the

46

past – the result of misunderstanding among themselves; they have – as soon as the evil agencies referred to above were removed – become as united and friendly as ever – therefore as a means to strengthen this union and friendly feeling among all classes. . .

THE THEATRE OF THE POEM GOES TO BLACK

*Kid, coming out of smoke, coughing, looking at something slightly behind him off
stage, claps haphazardly five times.*
Kid:

Mr. Pelletier, hey, there he is, there he
Yucked up, laughing, roll your own,
No teeth at all, swaying on his lonesome over prairie
Out of Lebret, crest-limping, brown as saskatoons, moving,
Is, moving, with a bag and a stick, by the cowherd Wascana,
To the dump, defrocked from the war,
Engineer in the Italian campaign,
Angled into that clown-guy Red Skelton did,
Tilted with a yuck, with a healed-over laughtrack, alone with his bag and stick,
Goaltending some beauty, gathering, no teeth, wild
Gardening old doll's carriage wheels,
Bearings, part of a budgie cage,
Half cans of paint.
The elms in Grassick Park slewed their eyes,
Hissing handful of seed,
With slick care, the
Act bottomlessly deniable,
(beautifully drinkable)
And beheld all that
Economy move through.
Poplars at St. Laurent
    (arrival of the saints):
Sun just up, netted to grass frost,
Hoofmarks, crow prints darkened into snow crumb.
The first wobbling monstrance quakes over
The erupted wall, the shivering armed priest,
The burnt church waits for them,
Charred pews nuzzling
Crows,
Crows crossing the bridge which
Trembles.
Fr. Noël-Joseph Ritchot and Big Bear and Mr. Pelletier and

Honoré Jaxon and
Piapot and others kingly in the hills,
The ladder, the figures shaking over
The burnt wood bridge,
Where they move, a sphere, the world.
Brown bales frozen to the field
Of to-the-knee, wintered timothy,
A bay of field curving into white trees.
St. Martin de Porres, swaying where a flag would be,
With sixteenth-century pills
And surgical knives, with a handful
Of pileated woodpecker feathers.
Jan Wyers bootlegs in with Mrs. Eugenie Lavallé
And Sr. Florence Leduc, Wyers driving a truck sidepannelled
With riveted sheet metal from Windthorst and dumps kindling in the yard.
Andy Suknaski rubs his new, pissed off beard along a crow's back
And hides out
In abandoned, talking-to-itself Wood Mountain
Below the pigeon shit collapsed roof of the Romanian church
And hears the wheel-groan of buffalo men
Trailing up from Rock Creek and
Passes, a perfect lateral, this news, pale nest of fire,
On up the way, cougar, to elk, to beaver, to crucifix-holding,
Casketed Charles Nolin
In the graveyard at Fish Creek.

Drums and cello played with vigour. Bull's Forehead Hill walks among the players,
raising his hands to quiet the instruments, horses circling with speed in a corral.

SEVENTH WATCH

Bull's Forehead Hill:

The red bruise of a mosquito

Cloud slides along trees

In a prairie chicken loincloth.

It carries a stonehammer,

It chips down stones to smaller stone.

The prairie is emptying out

Sara Riel:

Draining away.

Honoré Jaxon:

Drifting like water.

Bull's Forehead Hill:

As it did four thousand years ago.

Grasshoppers trade leaves for quills and coyote

Push their afternoons across a table for

A horn of snow piercing

The clay badland hill.

Cabri Effigy:

Edzizia obsidian,

Anahum obsidian.

Top of the World chert,

Knife River flint walked into

The Dakotas on feathered feet, walked

Into Cypress Hills, Rainy River

On painted legs of exchange,

Bijou hills copper,

Qu'Appelle red pipestone,

Smoke from the red valley

Under Grenfell, below the natural ice hockey rink. Shell

From the Gulf of Mexico,

Lake Superior copper shied

To the forks of the North and South

Saskatchewan, here, smell and masticate and frisk the ledger,

Kootenai argillite whistled into Alberta,

Yellowstone obsidian whistled in,

Montana chert put its shoes under the bed
Of the rise south of reeds and sedge, duck fields
West of the Missouri Coteau, a round
Of scrapers, Besant hill.
Flint from Tongue River, Flat Top chalcedony,
Orkeny fiddle, Smoky Hills jasper,
Pewter teapot, female spout,
From Birmingham, prie-dieu
From Rivière-du-Loup, lace shawl
From Fort Albany,
Nipigon copper laid out uncorrupted in a glacier's tongue
Near the headwaters of the Athabasca.
Riel:
Men come crawling to me two feet under the ground,
They've cladded themselves
With paving stones of prairie.
Trees wave on their backs like quills.
They come close enough to listen.
Here, let the calendric stone tower rise as it breathes,
Breathing from my mouth
An acropolis of attentive magpies.
That's what I'll say,
My speech, linking up before my face.
The moon rises grasshopper
Antennaed with scotch broom,
The moon guts out in stucco
From the acropolis' sides.
They threw me from a buffalo robe near Dumont's ferry
And as long as I floated
Above the skin trampoline
The country formed a sentence.
The winter count walked toward me
And took me in,
I was floating voice, growing hair, its penis hardening,
Thighs flashing ex votos,
Soaking up the sickness of all.

They came toward me, horses'
Hooves lifting great slabs
Of wind-packed snow.
Poplars:
Up and down the carboned rivers, along night's plated ears, along
Night's one facial horn, the Battle, Red
Deer, Carrot, North and South
Saskatchewans, Qu'Appelle, they crow hop
Around fires and open their packs
And break out and trade, and the *Critique of Judgement* goes
Into a cradle board
And is tied up tight and packed into Beauval area
Where its blackening hair will grow long
And those Ruth Cuthand drawings and the Kent Monkman
Blow-out at the Art Gallery of Greater Victoria
And that Susan Shantz installation Canopy, are laid across
Travois and scraped away, and the north star
Is dropped in a cup of poplar sap and the canoe glides on morning mist into
    the air
Of a living room south of Limerick, Saskatchewan. The cottonwood
Leaves clubbed yellow, rumble in
A northwest wind
And four beaver pelts gets you a little
Bit of haecceity
Served with a salad.
They rode on the prairie, horses
Utterance under them, naked as angels under them.
Gabriel poled the ferry around
Bleached September sandbars
Downstream from the winter camp.
He tied the ferry to horses' tails
And it moved across,
Black blade of ice, mane of ice, yielding
To soaked struts when the boat lipped up sand
And the horses docked.
And cranes were jumping in near fields

Five feet in the air,
Single feet extended soteriologically
Or arousedly in front of them.

Drums, cries, shots fired in the air. Sudden silence.

EIGHTH WATCH

Bull's Forehead Hill and Cabri Effigy, each taking a line. The speakers are inert,
slumped away from each other at the neck, while leaning back to back, before their
names are called from the darkened upper right of the stage, and they startle.

Fort Garry, 1869 *(good news)*
We stayed awake all one night with one lamp.
A single roughthroated lamp.
(They say these first lines in unison, turning toward each other, then, surprised, us.
Then alternate lines.)
Yes, then pintoed horses late the next afternoon brought letters *('clap)*
Of introduction through snow, seals with ribbons, perfectly *(clap)*
Honourable credentials, letters of wingbeats *(clap)*
From the shadow you see
When you look down through to streambed
On Rock Creek, below-water ledges of grass, south of Kildeer. *(clap, clap)*
Yes! Quite fine and calm letters of quill rattle, of claw drag
Through anthills,
Seals of hooves over stone. *(clap)* Yes!
To wrangle, arms raised, a love-place with the Dominion.
Yes, to deer-slot scrape out a love-place. *(clap)*
Americans rubbed a Fenian scent straight up poplars in Rupert's Land.
Shovels-for-sale, coke-muling Fenians
In from Miami, Buffalo,
Were still all night
Under the governor's bed in blood spray
At Fort Garry *(clap)*
As four winged dragonflies *(clap)*
Brought letters of saliva glue, *(clap)*
Credentials the colour of slate, *(clap, clap)*
Letters full of pine needles
To chinwag with the commotion, with railway yelling
Brit asslickers, to work a bunion for the onion, *(clap)*
Union with the nation,
And from Île-à-la-Crosse
A mink-soaked cloth

From Reindeer Lake pictographs
And a swan's wing,
From Willow Bunch and Milk River, feathers scraping
And pillowing along sandstone walls *(clap)*
To harness the palaver of the work that brought
Horse-whicker into fealty with a grey whale.
They'd been on the road a long time, they'd
Pounded thinking into proteined dust, squashed in
Lard and berries and took it in bearded parfleches
And that's what got them through. *(clap)*
They went out trading the grasshoppered crop of 1858 *(clap, clap, clap)*
At Red River for half
An hour of Milton Berle, early
Uncle Miltie, dressed as a woman, *(clap)*
Part of the pile, *(clap)*
Then sat down to intaglio a union with Canada
Jewellerying in personal shade
Their own quiet, souped-Catholic, ultramontane rings. *(clap)*
Ottawa, you're totally lost,
Smoking your cigars
Said the benignly loving horses
After they'd rested a bit around their mouth-scattered hay. *(clap, clap,*
    general laughter)
Poplars:
They traded some red cloth
To see Theoren Fleury moving sideways again in front
Of the net, moving sideways, no one else capable of this,
Two guys hanging on him,
In Salt Lake City,
Drop pass to Freddy Sasakamoose, here's some rehab.
And they traded a Dave Clark Five
45 for lamp oil and baleen.
And the older men packed pemmican twenty-six days
Out of Red River
To fatten an orb of quiet, horse-nervous
Quiet, risen in a grove of willows near Cache Creek

And on large stones gargling from the Carrot
They traded body-long strips of black
Cloth for an Orthodox sermon on
Ephesians that polished the claim angelic wisdom
Grew from attention to ecclesia
And they traded four yards of moving water
On Jack Elliot Creek for . . .
A quart of Drum River quiet for . . .
A 5:30 a.m. sun on Turtle Mountain for . . .
Bull's Forehead Hill (claps three times).
Reads the Declaration of Rights, 1885, French, English, Cree:
The Revolutionary Bill of Rights passed on March 8, 1885, St. Laurent,
  Saskatchewan
1. That the half-breeds of the Northwest Territories be given grants similar
   to those accorded to the half-breeds of Manitoba by the Act of 1870.
2. That patents be issued to all half-breed and white settlers who have fairly
   earned the right of possession on their farms.
3. That the provinces of Alberta and Saskatchewan be forthwith organized
   with legislatures of their own, so that the people may be no longer subject
   to the despotism of Mr. Dewdney.
4. That in these new provincial legislatures, while representation according
   to population shall be the supreme principle, the Metis shall have a fair and
   reasonable share of representation.
5. That the offices of trust throughout these provinces be given to residents
   of the country, as far as practicable, and that we denounce the appointment
   of disreputable outsiders and repudiate their authority.
6. That this region be administered for the benefit of the actual settler and
   not for the advantage of the alien speculator.
Clap, clap
And the morning was the breath of grass.
Cabri Effigy and Honoré Jaxon, alternating:
Concrescents in the hierarchy, nesting birds
In the star and flower ladders, bow and reach
To one another.
The grassblade sets out plates
And cups along Garry Oak leaves for the red moth

And the hummingbird brings
Fresh sheets and good coffee and pieces of ham
To the raccoon.
They are identified by lizards.
They are named by the rustling of frogs.
The purple above the first nodule
On long grasses' root ledgers in their afternoon
Movement-whisper across the sun, which it multiplies
By the power grid of grasshoppers.
The wasps lay out oats for the lightning stroke.
Women gather wild onions
Sew canoes with spruce root rope.
Winter worms in and smokes and pushes along rhizomes
Of frost which skin the mouth closed.
Mouths sweet with frost.
Pause
Sara Riel:
I didn't think you'd find
This fire back in these Missouri
Coulees.
Riel:
I followed some horses,
Two Appaloosa, rocks fallen from the sky,
I was running barefoot
Until the snow ended.
Pause. Rattle of tin camp equipment, sound of log thrown on the fire.
Sara Riel:
I got some tea,
Lots of sugar. Canned milk.
Bull's Forehead Hill:
First heavy snow in the foothills and Dall sheep
Hump down a hundred yards
Into the refugia of Assiniboia.
Three women come out to me, two sisters and a half-sister cousin
And sit for four days, no tents,
Not eating

And are in the refuge of Assiniboia.
A coyote pestering and picnicking around a Hutterite colony
Southwest of Maple Creek is in the gold-capped tooth
In the mouth of the
City of refuge.
The state comes from its coat, its wealth
Breathing, the bullion cache.
The state which is choir practice,
Its lands the angle of a voice
The way light builds a wave and falls through a voice.
The state is from the mouth and is the mouth.
Riel:
Through and out of blizzards somewhere
In the 1890s,
Gatling gun fired, shaking, Bigfoot frozen out in the filleted hills,
One eyelid of the ghost dance closed,
I danced two paths.
One to watch the ice tip then plunge in
The slack-quick green-brown South Saskatchewan River
The other to go into the white tail's coat
As a berry of melting snow.
Sara Riel:
And here you are. Here
Is a slice of frozen muskrat
Oblate (coming out of the dark):
That was a while back
What you remember, Louis.
It feels like soot on lampglass.
Sara Riel:
I was in a wind decades where blood
Sailed and snapped at the end of whips;
A buffalo locomotive cloud exploded
Blood from blowholes.
All that waiting
Snow slanting in jackpine
Smell of pelts carved from animals

Stacked in poplar sheds
Beside the creaking March lake.
Then I slid down the south bank
Of the White Mud.
Riel:
The body-temperatured milky thinking grunted us
From between its knees
Great jellyfish of mentation
Sara Riel:
We were dreamed around.
I got to know the intimate fold
Of feathers in the wing
And recognize and nod to the ripple in its rush.

SONGS OF CLARITY
IN FINAL PROCESSION

A SONG OF CLARITY

Dionysos, a waver of arms, the Stranger, unfurls his body from tumult

Earthquake swarms 250 miles into the Pacific –
Black World War II courier motorcycles
Pummel and well in pine silos – and they open
Whiskery mouth pouches of Queen Anne's lace on the peninsula, then elongate
Licorice fern tips with the stain of their sound.
Binding and fountaining,
They whuff the backside of teleology then ride out
On banana backs of their ascending teeth.
Three hundred floor offices of water.
I have been conducted to a cave of sun and declared wealthy
And seated before the loaned silver tea service of sanity.
Gored by the banks, my underwear on loan.
I see I've a little something to say to Sara Riel.
Frizzing as if damagedly wired,
It hovers, purple jellyfish, purple
Incandescent fork of gas over this, all we stare at.
The new land smelling of gasoline.
And in each of its corners is a god with a perfect eye,
And I believe we are herded by these eyes.

Our Lord Odysseus, the Traveller, timekeeping, rising, taking his shape from the
cauldron of his calculations

Origen, Origen, out of Alexandria, confused, afflicted in the fir,
Foreign ears cloved to him,
Bears and Origen out of decayed day clear-cut
Achieve the ridge, November bears, sudden black door of them
Studded with blow-whitened spikeheads of alertness,
Dipping down,
And they intercept the nineteenth century.
Origen works an exegesis down to its skeleton,
Dragon of the years,
And slides in a word like a titanium rod.
John Climacus and his trembling ladder of lamentation. Weep.
Origen, armoured with his upper arm of eyes,
Origen, made a seal by hearing.
There's a white volcano across the water; it's immediately keen
And leans in. Look back. The Industrial Revolution
Coloured creek drops and tears.

Alders on a bank like crushed asphalt.
The creek, an antibiotic coma,
Someone reciting the names of everyone
Who lived in a completely burned city.

Odysseus, the Weeper, walking away, speaking without turning his head, homed and
mealed in the chant, swinging a stick through grass

Naming and numbering
The taxonomic fall and curves of Lights,
Their warm bellyings out of love, lumbering, weight-building hums, he was
By Mill Creek, upstream from the drying cement bridge as poplar buds
Disgorge beaky fans and peelings of snow
Nurse out in trees above
The creek and deer and elk and coyote and bear
Scat writes on the trails, white hair in the last, and moles
Corn-row up new loaves of earth.
Suhrawardi in strips of bluishly whipped light.
The fire's potbellied coals,
Another log flops on, ash achieves a crown of fire on its own dirt.
Smoke in hair and heavy, peaty coats,
The first grass worries out.
The dominating lights — incorporeal lights
Free of connections with barriers — are more
In number than a hundred thousand.
Some among them cause no independent barrier
For the individual independent barriers are fewer
In number than the stars and are ordered in rank . . .
And Mill Creek slickers into Castle Creek
Which tangles its horns into the rabbit-brown
Old Man and is raised up, lifted by its horns.
Something riding the stars, fields
Of cattle inside that flame.
Someone starts the tractor, a JD with a hay-claw,
To haul bales to still-wintering, bleary cows
Sweeping through hoofblackend old feed.
Light's white water, May 23rd.

AVICENNAN RECITAL (A SPIRITUAL TOPOGRAPHY)

Suhrawardi, in a coulee, reciting upward against the northeast wall

In one climate there are humans
Plated with rounds an inch deep
Of impacted feathers, wrapped by wide strips
Of reed, towhee, and hairy woodpecker feathers mostly
But also hummingbird gorget.
They do have "homes."
These are pods for sleeping
Made from pushing up lithic and bone and molar
Debris and spreading a layer of ash from a fresh fire
For sleeping into the lower half of this shell.
In another clime there are only quick movements,
People small, getting smaller;
And in another there is a Queen.
Six cities in that locale, each with a booming flag,
Then a band where people are slow as insects after a light frost
And love writing. They have ten cities.
In another, nothing, a big desert, some mountains,
Then a place of solitaries, huge land; it is like the display
Of a sage grouse, or the raised neck of a Roosevelt elk.
Then you leave the Occident
And there are floodplains,
I mean cobble washes at the edges of glaciers,
Then from between a set of horns, a flying man,
A viper with a boar's head.
Then a shadeline princedom of those that hatch
Those that crawl.
Then there are demons.
Then a satrapy of terrestrial angels;
There is mostly sandhills, red head triangles of the cranes, in this locus.
Another zone will be both thick and light
As if the air itself were labial folds or

Eyelids of smokeless flame.
There you will meet him,
The Garbiel-sword, the Angel, he looks, eyes below your cheekbones,
You open, then he becomes your closest meat,
A bed of nearness to you
Oval of pollen under thy skin.
This is its government.
The arrow of your beauty
Entering you
Above, they say, the left nipple.

Narrator, standing, rocking, side to side, eyes closed, on a snow-covered low mountain,
overlooking the town

The tradition which had tempered the persons in Frost's poems had
already, before the Civil War, sung its last high Word in the old terms
that were valid from Plato to Fichte. And this too was fitting, for the
Civil War prepared the doom which the World War completed, of our
agrarian class-culture. But the great tradition, unbroken from Hermes
Trismegistus and Moses, does not die.
      — Waldo Frank, Introduction to Hart Crane's "The Bridge," 1932

Let it be more drunken,
Let there be a watery room, fringed
With auric dust,
Waste of hearing,
Tailings of hearing's big show.
In the Ridgeview Motor Inn,
Edge of the claw, sea digging
Through its sock drawer,
$59 a night, loggers moaning, chaining their boots, tolling,
Above, below, grey whales in the straits, crowbarring north,
Corporate rate for the hesychast,
Long breather, his ear, on manoeuvres, an eddy
Tight as a curl on the forehead of Elizabeth I.

In a watery room with a golden, fur-like
Waving, drinking edge, the sea grows to the side of his head,
Rubbery like tree fungus.
What use will this be, map of Belgian Congo, circa 1883?
Bring, Sweet Force of Luck, the whip of exegesis.
He hooks in, tars down, tongue

And grooves, spruce strip sews in a sloppy, smacking, full elk-heave,
Touchdown roar, of antler,
Dish of the curving whole,
And the counting of breaths becomes a jeweller's saw
He cranks back and forth on the foot
Of this moneyed spurt of ghost.

Thousand-watt lamps cook snow
In fringes from peoples' houses.
You hear electricity's crinkle
Rub through dark's plush,
Plants neck flare, crawl their faces across glass
With spark-like latex squeaks.
Inside an auric teardrop, which rents
The room, someone, pseudo–Isaac of Ninevah, under the table,
Counts his breaths,
Landed prayer hacking into him, clinging as magnetized hair.

—#—

Erratics, ditch water frozen,
Down the pass in, a few reeds, rain drag, rain scruff hatting coal
Heaps and troll-nosed mountains,
Road to Tahsis in axel-high snow,
They all turn back, electricity, barely knapped, penstocking
Into the town a slither of knives on knives
In night's fur.
River thrash and river slag, fog
Goatishly circling and sniffing
The anus of Mount Baldy.
The teeth in the chain,
The gear in the forest's blackberries.
Water slabs off
Monstrously slanted shale.

Through the break-up of the satellite phone,
He reaches the bridge of the *Uchuck III* and learns
This is how it stands: they won't take him, the breather, on the black boat
Unless he finds a sleeping bag, appendix of a home.
No, actually, no room for him on the non-skin working ship
Fevering up the coast into fir and night.
The weeper sleeps where he is.
Now the sea pulls its stomach out beyond the inside passage,
They cannot sail to Kyuquot.

Sara Riel

The water tusks off the mountain,
Exhausted, celibate,
With a single eye.
Fog waddles, sea lion, to mill this eye
Into something useful,
Dark kernel of its katabasis
To black bread
But the heavy wheel has pitted away
Half an inch from impact.
The eye berry rejoices in itself.
Now it can enter the library below buttresses
Of oak root and consider the far-flung code
Like blown cities under all skin
And receive the infinitely bendable antenna
From which courses the right tongue.
And here, in husky sobriety, the complete human body inside water
Finds the quilted gaze of Marguerite Porete
And it draws the cloth of that attention
Through its savouring hands.

Odysseus and Suhrawardi, a duet, anything you can do, I can do much better

O: Like Turtle Mountain, I am a third fallen away.
S: Like Turtle Mountain, I have blanket-stacked melancholia
within grains of matter that have no virtue to grow their own,
      wrenches at old mine sites, their hand-blackened ends;
                  new poplar; limestoned towns.
O: With the odourless sun, I see to Bolshevik(!) Winnipeg;
I walk down a street; I order a triumphant meal, radiant chicken!;
I talk to the bronze-armed Christians there about a silver, kissed
vaulting over labour at the workface of belief;
      the dolphin-breaching tongue, I say. Just go after it
                        and drift my hand like a scarf.
S: I have seen Iamblichus with a herd of goats
on the northeast forehead and jaw of Turtle Mountain.
Iamblichus had a jelly-like yet gorgeously transparent abdomen,
he was in the shape of a wasp, light
went through him like two warehouses of arrows.
The train hissed through the pass below me.
O: Like Turtle Mountain, I can see to where my wife is
in High River, living with "uncles" as an imaginary shoal,
Sophie Christiansen Shoal, in the middle of the South Ocean of the Pacific.
S: I take out the rainforest of the dictionary,
put my nose in the gutter, and by the lamp of my sunken body
see coal ferns below the forest, cedar thick under the steaming floor,
and I motion to animals there in the heavy-stomached pit
and like house-big millipedes, like
giant sloths, they do come out, darlings, and move
apatheia, fish-quiver of emptiness,
anachoresis, the genius of withdrawal, the cave bear's
sense of order, and here we have a new world.

O: The knapped face I am after to scrape out these poems
doesn't come out of Africa but only out of Central Asia.
S: Like Turtle Mountain, I can see the dust of events
rising as they smoke up, leave and come.
Here is singularity itself, of all things,
can't be more than 125 chimed pounds,
on one of the horses of the passion of God,
weaving from the last barely sloped bed of water
with flowering saskatoons in the east.
O: Like Turtle Mountain, I can see from here the naked back
of Rebecca Belmore, the S-shaped scar
from her right shoulder to the top of her hips,
with its buckskin of hanging surgical threads
red white red.

(after Mahmoud Darwish)

EGYPTIAN BOAT

Louis Riel

> The age quiets down, culture goes to sleep, a people is reborn having
> given its best forces to a new social class; and this whole current bears
> the frail boat of the human word into the open sea of the immediate
> future . . . . How can one rig this boat for its distant trek, without
> having supplied it with everything necessary for so alien and so precious
> a reader? Once more I compare the boat to an Egyptian boat of the
> dead. In this boat everything is equipped for life; nothing is forgotten.
>   – Osip Mandelstam, "About the Nature of the Word"

This is of breath, breath, breath, breath
to its curved end, canoe-ish, a cherubimic contract, starry trireme, burnt
from cedar, slapped with edged stone; it is piled with honeycomb slabs,
cylinders of water genuine and swift, handmirrors and combs, talkative
breasts, word-bread, wheat in fields at rest, night,
basket-ready willow stems, breath, breath,
breath, exegetes, July whorls in air, sausage,
Athenian dust, loose hay, multiple languages, fine
shirts with lines of pink in them.

Lipscooped is the boat of thick leather and memory, whisky-crates,
long feathers fatherly, wrenches, tie-wire, electricity, cunning and
        counting,
counting.
It moves. It moves across the teeth,
it drags you and angles you into soil.
An engine that chaffs in a worn mist of metaphysics
riding up coulees in southwest Saskatchewan.
It has a wet ground smell.
The poem, the Egyptian boat, the poem, its gear, winch.
An axial word stands red, bellying, at
the centre, scrape it with a knife

and from the mouth of that nounpole shining
will-lavas picnics, television
                    seepage light,
bear tracks, shoulders of meat.

The boat, a snowplough-pushing up, mouth-hoarding, travels
though moistly over and will, will, I guarantee,
carry anyone through tall buildings
throwing horns of energy into arctic air in Calgary
in the encyclopedic end of night,
fire-nicked stories, acting like metal slivers or quartz
pins, Christian and eighteenth century, holding the cold
longer, very much longer, in the skin of us, while
the tar pit gutters down northwest of Cold Lake
where is mined Urgency and Pressing
and snakes appear on the sour muskeg floor and in pines.
Choice's liposuction carves the sag from things
but the boat is untouched.

Sara Riel

Raspberry flower, raspberry flower, raspberry flower,
their red bees, broken off the earth's long stalk
itself, the heavy rocket of earth falling away behind, bees trailing
                          smoke of pneuma, bees of
ore-cunning, bees of simmering, of stunned centrality
shaking like the tip of the semi's quivering floor joy stick,
potato-odoured, elementish
bees.
Raspberry flower, raspberry flower,
     spiritual excreta, exact minute picnics, clotted embroidery, new lands,
          the purity of France!
The bees are noonish, monadic, noongong, are insect-taxis
poking through beeead-da-da-ded curtains
of the lightly knotted white faces of hair
of raspberry flower, looking for the passage, the fair, the, of course,
raspberry flower vault, the
struck face of the flower, the bankable, rumbling mousecoat
                          of the beeeee
eeee. Raspberry flower, raspberry flower, raspberry flower, raspberry
flower, the bees' drawl and the twang and the trailer-
          parkery of the bees,
their blow-tremours shivering down the stalk.

                    (after Ferenc Juhász)

PORT RENFREW

Honoré Jaxon, speaking in immurement, living in Osprey Cabins, in the aftermath

> Either the human community must offer a structure in which
> esoterism is an organic component; or else it must suffer all the
> consequences implied by a rejection of esoterism.
> — Henry Corbin, *Creative Imagination in the Sufism of Ibn 'Arabi*

Water smoke,
San Juan Basin coal cloud,
Emergency brake released,
Metal on metal, somnambulant,
Shears forward, stunting,
Piano pushed from a fifth-floor room,
To jellyingly become our walls
That halibut talk through,
Oil bulge of their voices rolling under lids.
November's rain axe falls,
Falls and dresses our homes
In quick-lit gowns
Of each stroke's fury and polish.

Unconcealment – through
The genitaled walls through
Whose lozenges the speech
Of fish appears, wakes, collapses, wakes,
Wakes much farther out, then skin-rustles closed.

Cross the road to the guy running
The cappuccino machine.
Cedar wows and swords
Below knee air, chiselling toward light
In hard, not really thinkable seeds,

77

Cutting away what the lumen front requires
To rise, mustardseedly deranged or enraged –
Spiked beings on the backs of horses
Of clouded spark –
To near
The mouth of aggregate air.

The 20 kph turn slewed me out
Flying over missiles of trees,
The coast, bad god teeth,
    up to the shouldery fog before
The seal-raisoned ice.
Small caves in the air
To look from, thinking.

Like Osprey Cabins, #2, here, working out, unplying, sequentially
Sara Riel and *Timaeus*
Inside an oval pit house
Scraped into rain, in basaltic reading glow.
These two, these two;
They could be moving now through trees
On deer legs.

ANTIPHON

> When he had finished with his speech, he turned again to the mixing
> bowl he had used before, the one in which he had blended and mixed
> the soul of the universe. He began to pour into it what remained of
> the previous ingredients ...
>
> — *Timaeus* 41e

Drums and cello briefly reappear. They stop.
Hermocrates steps forward from a stand of fir at the end of night; he appears
speaking, hissing to a group assembled around Socrates.

Hermocrates:
Because of what you are
We have been awake all night with your question about the city and the city
    at war.
How could we offer what you'd said
In the unsteady flame of actual motion?
The film of the sea, a feature of the entire afterlife,
Shudders in eaten sprockets.
The ocean reams freight cars of clause after clause
To deepen a bore in the sound, far out, the northern straits
Skate rollingstock
And these disintegrate, rotting from several yards in,
From the ore-beyond-imagination spider-wrapped in them,
Cree sentences, Thomas Carlyle sentences, Peter Lomb. . . .
I met someone outside Critias' quarters
Who can stand behind, wrestler in a suit, completely what I saw.
Weight-of-the-world water — bushels and skeins
Of palaces, treatises, all a barbelled thing, deep
Uranium mines, softball fields of sex —
It gouges grasshopper coloured down the rock ledge.
This ocean, north, the trench's book,
The water reciting in its iron shirt,

The water raises its grey-tipped ash shafts
Folding over the berm in many and against the cliff,
Where a rust blue Mazda quarter-ton hoves against my landlord's paint-boiled
House, that swims dank around the furious bowl.
Continent edge, crystal meth cabanas, Sitka
                                        spruce, a machine
Of fog whirring its blades in alders.
The ocean upends and fans and fans its stone-black sayings book
Scraping from the bottom of this codex
Cooked on gobbets of meat,
Scraping, scraping, the ocean,
In its beards, its grooving paranoia,
Calling out its protections, its protections,
Its protections, its protections.
The water is never finished.
It sweeps and cleans and draws its black
Blood from its arm, rolling bed of bulls, and tweezers the blood
Between burnt matches
And reads the blood looking down the tunnel with its swaying stair.
The ocean's sword-dust, multiple sayings, its self-sprainings,
Unelected doublings back, ash curves
On a cigarette, piling too long, towering
Too long.

So this stranger, you'll have heard this, yes?, creeps up in The Water's Edge
Or The Trail's End Tavern, hoarfrosted, the man,
With mathematical knowledge,
And says hairy people were made like jam
In a bowl with this ocean, the
Trench's book, this ocean in its iron war shirt,
Reading itself aloud, aloud. Loud, the water's
Bear ruff, the night's seal cloak.
Rustles like the mic-ed vestments of Orthodox, seal-smooth priests
Shoulder-padded with incense,
Moving in log churches smoky with vermin.

Amplified shot silk, scraping.
This place cranks its dial for Alaska, which rubs its crotch for Siberia.
Otter furs, cruelty and asceticism. That's the burnt taste
Below the tuck of the tongue,
How it's rounded the skin inside the mouth with its heats.
The water confesses everything sideways; darkness is itself;
It has no Luciferean charm or guile.
Where is the guile in two reefer loads sideswiping the full one hundred feet
In the Strathconas on the Campbell River Road?
The ocean is the bigbellied steel of theogenesis and its perpetuation,
                                    flopping down,
Digging in, then scudding back to the simple air, knives, horn cutting
Wire, maces,
Steel golf balls spurred all around.
The sea with its arms pulled off
By its own brief handshakes.
The many-bulled water, the many bulls
Of water collapse and throw out
Their telescopic wings in rasping unison,
The ground of water pounded feedlot black.
The water a volcanic sleigh pulled by wolves.

—#—

The golden, golden soul,
Can you believe it, the sent-man
Hacking in the bar, flipping and spinning
His double cheese voice, throwing salt
Over his shoulder, crest of salt, onto the reptile gnarled indoor outdoor
Of what was it the Quiney, The King George,
Can't call it up,
His politbureaun Breznevian flag-face snapping over the beer,
Was freshened, he said, winged, when the scented Father
Studying the Living Thing blowhorned
The weaker gods, "I shall begin
By sowing a superb seed, big as a pickled egg, and then hand it over
To you."

And then he spun around with what was it
A cleaver, a marmorealean dart, bluey, whaleish, no,
Wait, bat-coloured, bat-coloured, in his hand,
No, no, what am I thinking, an exact, perilous, frog-faced rock
And he squared to the same waxing, bronco-ing bowl
In which he'd piledriven the asteroid and conked and mashed together
The Motions, the Motions, the Motions,
The Motions of things, rammed to stick to one another, Sun and Moon
Shining the last like a tusk, of course, Fire
Sweated from rapid change,
Like horses or antelope, which were not
Yet,
And there were bits of the skin of these still inside, spit-spackled,
Stuck to the edge, electron mucus,
Not the best, lunks, locks, a bit of tooth, could have been, maybe,
A cracked button from a ceremonial coat,
Second or third grade of purity,
And he pounded and chaffed again and there it was, overmattered ellipses,
Inside, from the Sun, from the Air, nude, absolutely, with certainty,
Fleshing lightly from its own roar, the soul,
In shocks of tail-rotoring, forcing foam.

The ocean played with its broken arm,
Spinning, a blizzard over a one-hundred-square-mile section
Of it, moved and moved, night soaked into it, night
Shanked its body into the water.

ACKNOWLEDGEMENTS

I thank Ken Babstock, my editor, for his assistance in the last stages and those who read the manuscript in earlier versions and offered valuable advice: Jan Zwicky, Helen Marzolf, Warren Cariou, Sue Sinclair, Warren Heiti, Don McKay, Don Domanski, Cara-Lyn Morgan, Carolyn Forché, Robin Poitras, and Louise Halfe.

I have consulted many histories of Riel and the two governments that were attempts to enact Assiniboia. The most helpful were *Riel: A Life of Revolution*, by Maggie Siggins; *Honoré Jaxon*, by Donald B. Smith, and *To Louis from Your Sister Who Loves You, Sara Riel*, by Mary Jordan. The fragments of the story in Cree in the "Second Watch" of the masque come from *Sacred Stories of the Sweet Grass Cree*, collected by Leonard Bloomfield in 1925. The story of Flute-Bearer was told to Bloomfield by Coming-Day (kâ-kîsikâw-pîhtokêw).

Earlier forms of some of the poems appeared in *Grain, The Malahat Review, Hobo, Eleven Eleven* (United States), *The Goose, Best Canadian Poetry: 2010, Contemporary International Poetry: Canadian Poetry Special Edition* (China).